Pin Pricks

For Andrew

Pin Pricks

Phlip Arima

QUATTRO BOOKS

The publication of *Pin Pricks* has been generously supported by the Canada Council for the Arts and the Ontario Arts Council.

Canada Council for the Arts Conseil des Arts du Canada

ONTARIO ARTS COUNCIL
CONSEIL DES ARTS DE L'ONTARIO
50 YEARS OF ONTARIO GOVERNMENT SUPPORT OF THE ARTS
50 ANS DE SOUTIEN DU GOUVERNEMENT DE L'ONTARIO AUX ARTS

Cover image: Thomas Hendry
Cover design: Sarah Beaudin
Editor: Allan Briesmaster
Typography: Grey Wolf Typography

The author wishes to thanks Angela Aitken and Clara Blackwood for their friendship and support; and Thomas Hendry for the cover image.

Library and Archives Canada Cataloguing in Publication

Arima, Phlip, author
Pin pricks / Phlip Arima.

Poems.
ISBN 978-1-927443-57-6 (pbk.)

I. Title.

PS8551.R762P56 2014 C811'.54 C2014-901594-1

Published by Quattro Books Inc.
Toronto
info@quattrobooks.ca
www.quattrobooks.ca

Printed in Canada

Pin Prick 1

As each illusion fades
I know less than I thought
and am more than I was.

Pin Prick 2

A personality drips
from the edge of my mouth
it covers my body
hides my pulse.

Pin Prick 3

Naked
I walk to the wall
count the cracks
that disappear
into the floor.

Listening
I hear a siren
screaming toward
a greater
drama.

Pin Prick 4

Every day ten thousand children are hidden
in electronic folders, insurance policies
are lottery tickets, a prison-orange sky
sweats a promise.

Calculator and clock both run on the same
disposable batteries, a good morning kiss
is forgotten by noon, painkillers
can be found in every
bedroom.

Pin Prick 5

At the circus
I let my balloon
go

heads turned
fingers pointed

I wonder why
no one cheered.

Pin Prick 6

The power fails
the city goes dark.

The stars that fill the sky
look far farther away
than they do on television.

Children cling to their parents
hyperventilate, tremble
cry.

Pin Prick 7

Normal is a measure
not a goal.

Pin Prick 8

I build a pretty sandcastle
with simple solid walls
two roads leading to its gate
a candy wrapper for a flag.

I imagine rooms filled with treasure
romancing couples in every tower
a happy king dancing and singing
parents playing with their child.

I love the tapestries in the great hall
know every one of its secret tunnels
hide in the deepest when the shouting
gets too loud.

Pin Prick 9

The gerbil runs across the floor
in its translucent plastic ball

a hollow sphere rolling over toes
hitting heels, bouncing off walls

racing through every open door
always hyper, forever separate.

Pin Prick 10

I sell my spoon, my pot, my knife
for a handful of uncooked rice.

Pin Prick 11

Abandoned trousers in the street
a young face at a window
someone waves an ancient flag
a glass of wine falls over.

A line of cars run out of gas
bets are placed on politicians
dogs are freed from a kennel.

A summer storm destroys a city
soldiers put their helmets on
debates are staged for television.

Sticks of incense near an altar
lose their scent to time.

Pin Prick 12

I sip from her glass
taste every flavour
she has known

touch her face
feel each pore
heat

wait
for her to smile.

Pin Prick 13

Another statement made with blood
turns to dust in mid-day heat.

Throughout the afternoon and night
anger burns through tightening veins.

At dawn more blood is violently spent
to send a reply, provoke a response.

Pin Prick 14

Restrained compassion
is a candle without flame.

Pin Prick 15

The streetcar stops
the crowd sways
straightens.

Someone coughs.

Grips relax
shoulders sag
unconnecting eyes
stare.

The floor vibrates.

A phone rings and
we all get to listen
to half
a conversation.

Pin Prick 16

Just inside your crystal ball
I take off my clothes, close
my eyes, know you wait
for me to dance.

I lift my feet, move my arms
sway to dreams you've not
imagined

until your breath
fogs the glass.

Pin Prick 17

Two men of different skin
talking as they walk
down the street.

An obscenity is shot
from a passing car.

They pause, sigh
never stop holding hands.

Pin Prick 18

The acrobats spin together, apart
dynamic awareness inherent
in every moment.

Astounded
the man beside me
spills his drink down my leg.

Pin Prick 19

Wet with summer sweat
needing a haircut
I watch a tree
drop its leaves
to the pavement beyond
its concrete box.

Pin Prick 20

Exhaust smogs the window
a light burns out, the screen-saver
continues its silent routine.

I pick up the phone, stare at the
numbers, try to remember
why.

There's a wall in the next room I've been
meaning to paint, dishes in the kitchen
that need to be replaced.

I put the phone down, open
the window, watch a small bird
fly into traffic.

Pin Prick 21

Students take notes
scholars make notes.

Pin Prick 22

I hang a picture on the wall
step into its frame and wonder
how I once saw its illusion of depth
as any different from the reality I left.

Pin Prick 23

Your hand
resting on my sex
has been comfortably still
for longer than I
can remember

while your other hand
exploring within mine
caressing deeper
possibilities
thrills.

Pin Prick 24

When all the music
is too loud
and all the dancers
have passed out
I turn my cell phone
off

hope a new song
will be written
unimagined
chords played.

Pin Prick 25

Demolition dust
and construction dirt
cover my window
like a shroud.

The plants on the sill
are not happy: one has lost
nearly all its leaves, another
has turned yellow, curled in
on itself.

My favourite
has withered
beige.

Pin Prick 26

In the long rays
of the late day sun
a shadow lies behind me
while another
invisible to the eye
but possible to glimpse
with an unfettered mind
stretches from my toes
to a place I will
never know.

Pin Prick 27

Fresh water and rice
some peas for protein.

Tonight the children
will sleep quiet.

Pin Prick 28

The advanced guard gets shot down
the troops that follow conquer.

Pin Prick 29

Snakes that constrict their prey
do not bruise or break the bones
of their victims. Organs
are not crushed. Skin
is never cut.

Constrictors simply
slowly steadily squeeze
until the trapped
cannot breathe.

Celebrity interviews
tell me everything
I need to know.

Pin Prick 30

Your castle knocks my queen
from the board, blue sky
is revealed by fleeing
clouds, each leaf
of every plant
turns toward
the window.

The computer
automatically
resets
the music.

You ask if I still
want to play.

Pin Prick 31

Each day the bombs get closer
their volume more intense.

Each night we turn the music louder
swallow a larger drink.

Pin Prick 32

I chip the wax from a tarnished candlestick
reveal bright brass to the afternoon sun
look for meaning in the shining shapes.

A fan moves the air above my head
a fly crawls up the window
the refrigerator makes
its usual noise.

I polish the candlestick
until its surface
is all the same.

Pin Prick 33

The body remembers
the shrieks
and the
moans
buried within
each layer of skin
locked mute in flesh
bone marrow
breath.

Pin Prick 34

I see her sitting
in a high window
on the floor
back to the wall
cheek against the
dirty glass

I wonder her name
story, thoughts
so wave
and wait
for a response

like yesterday
tell myself
tomorrow will
be different.

Pin Prick 35

Fashion is conformity
style statement.

Pin Prick 36

I step out of bed
stumble on a statistic
fall through a commercial
climb into a corn popper
wait on hold.

I eat petals from a flower
once pressed in a book
write a blog on the dirt
between my toes
become a commodity
swallow a pill
watch an ice cube melt
in an ocean.

When I go on-line
I don't know what name
to use.

Pin Prick 37

He salutes a lie
he has always believed

raises his rifle
to sustain a myth

swears he will shoot
if so ordered.

Pin Prick 38

Last season's cool is discounted
everyone speaks of tomorrow's potential
a young face forgets how to smile.

Pin Prick 39

She says, I'm only
just learning to draw
not yet good at all.

Still, I know for sure
a self-portrait by her
would look lovely

on any one
of my waiting
walls.

Pin Prick 40

There's a crack in the floor
that lengthens each time
I step over it.

Its edges resemble
a cut on my hand
that will not heal.

Into it I've swept
the names I no longer
write on my calendar.

Pin Prick 41

Music from the bar below
shouts and laughter from the street
television from an apartment down the hall.

I watch a spider crawl across the ceiling
slide a metre down a thread
curl in on itself.

Remembering a lullaby
I clench my teeth.

Pin Prick 42

At the top of the roller-coaster
there is an empty stretch of time
where my pulse is put on hold
and every thought eats itself
as I gaze across the fair
at all the animated people
far too far away to hear
the crucial questions
I repeatedly
ask.

Then the ride begins.

Pin Prick 43

A fantasy realized
is a dead dream.

Pin Prick 44

I cannot
reach
the knife
in my back
despite the fact
the fingerprints
on the hilt
are mine.

Pin Prick 45

Bright lights follow her ascent
as she twists and turns the silk
around her muscled limbs

rising up from pose to pose
until cocooned high above
the crowd

then down she tumbles
toward the ground
stopping just

before she hits.

Pin Prick 46

Obsessive desire
distorts judgment

whispered envy
snuffs a candle

unvoiced screams
disembowel.

Pin Prick 47

A dozen
conversations
around half
as many tables
speaking of things
I don't understand.

A fire alarm rings
every voice gets louder.

I alone
leave.

Pin Prick 48

The soft scent of fine incense
quiets the voice that growls doubt
at every endeavour
I consider.

In a drawer beneath my bed is a picture
of a tree that no longer flowers
surrounded by light
green saplings.

A few steps from where I sit
are brush and ink and
a pristine sheet
of paper.

Pin Prick 49

We meet in an artificial womb
I'm watching the news
you change the channel

music videos pattern the walls
we dance on each other's skulls
thoughts melt into the floor
our skin dissolves.

When I google love
you can't stop laughing.

Pin Prick 50

Superstars are a poor substitute
for heroes.

Pin Prick 51

The tortoise was fully evolved
before mankind existed.

There are trees that have outlived
civilizations.

Just prior to the Second World War
we split the atom.

Pin Prick 52

I hold my heart in my hand
uncurl my fingers
watch it beat.

I question my feelings
the heart rolls over
falls to the street.

Pin Prick 53

A broken glass on the table
yesterday's love on the sheets

a whisper is screamed
a shout is silenced

flesh bruising
shame.

Pin Prick 54

My back aches from standing
straight, black water shrinks
my shoes

I keep my eyes open, but grind
my teeth, news reports are
limited to one hundred
forty characters

everywhere I turn I see a social
cripple, the bartender shouts
last call, an abandoned rose
falls to the floor.

Pin Prick 55

I cross the bumpy parking lot
to watch the shiny cars race by
beyond the fence that keeps me here.

I hold my littlest dolly up
so she can see the empty buildings
where my daddy used to work.

My favourite show was on today
where the fuzzy animals
fight the scary monster

over and over
and over
again.

Pin Prick 56

Words have become sounds
without any meaning:
noise we make
when not
alone.

Specific repetitions
guarantee response
the rest are hardly
noticed.

Jets high in the sky
seem to be silent
I wonder where
they go.

Pin Prick 57

The struggle to take off the armour
can be greater than every battle.

Pin Prick 58

I watch five cranes
from my window
moving earth
into the sky
building a world
that can be resold
repeatedly
until torn down
for something we
will believe
is better.

Pin Prick 59

The puppet cuts its strings
spits at the audience
continues the play
exactly as written.

Pin Prick 60

A slow hand
slides down
my body

pulls me out
of myself

before turning
to a claw

intent
on leaving scars

beauty
cannot diminish.

Pin Prick 61

Rain slick pavement dark
wet skin cold numb
lock clicks door open
soft light dry
quiet warm
sigh.

Pin Prick 62

Most pedestals
are very high
and looking down
causes vertigo
and falling
which always
inevitably happens
only stops
when the person
looking up
is crushed.

Pin Prick 63

Alone, I push through
a crowded club in shoes
a one-off left behind

reach into an abandoned
drink, steal the ice for
between my legs

listen to an electronic voice
approve my call for yet
another pseudonym

shape my mouth into
a grin, feel my lips
start to crack.

Pin Prick 64

Random acts of kindness
tend to blind.

Pin Prick 65

In the small bright room
we spoke of politics
and entertainment

as we spoke
I stood and shaved
while she sat and shit

then we switched positions.

Pin Prick 66

Like a whisper echoing over eons
touching those who cherish intimacy
the heart beats an unbroken rhythm
promises bliss, confuses
gives.

Pin Prick 67

I pull a file
across a nail
that will again
grow
and eventually
break.

Yesterday
I chose to dress
rather than welcome
the quiet.

Pin Prick 68

My tongue bleeds
when I speak
of love

my eyes
like traps
shut

blind bleeding
I stay when I
should flee.

Pin Prick 69

Green tea to heat the cold rice
leftover fish, raw
vegetables

disorientation recedes
thoughts return
promise

hope.

Pin Prick 70

Hanging from a chain
at the base of my throat
a locket conceals
an innocent expression
I stole from a child
on a merry-go-round.

Pin Prick 71

Moving through
a darkening room

with every thought
the floor expands

each time I blink
more pictures fill

the walls.

Pin Prick 72

You can't smell the flowers
when you're pushing them up.

Pin Prick 73

A seed gets trapped
in pavement crack.

A tender sprout
reaches for the sun.

Mighty roots
shift man-made stone.

Pin Prick 74

The elephant rolls over
and everyone applauds.

He stands on one leg
and everyone applauds.

He shits as he is leaving
and everyone pretends

not to notice.

Pin Prick 75

Noise-filled room
cold stone floor
ceiling too high
to see.

I sit with my hands
under my feet
wait for the pain
in my body to cease.

A silent cartoon
projected on the wall
flickers and slips
out of focus.

Pin Prick 76

I wait for a break in the traffic
my joints grow arthritic
hair hides my face.

The chocolate I swallow
is constantly replaced.

Pin Prick 77

My fingers grow numb
the book leaves my hand
hits the floor

words bounce from the pages
scatter flat syllables
across the tiles

they settle in the dust
wait to be swept up.

Pin Prick 78

Back-to-back we stand
first-love memories
between us.

You watch the sun rise
I, the moon set.

Forward we march
apart.

Pin Prick 79

Night sky
lightning lit

face distorted
with fading hope

thunder overwhelms
the plea in my voice

fingers touch
tear-wet lips.

Pin Prick 80

The painter makes brush strokes
I see a picture.

Pin Prick 81

Surrounded by noise
I retreat into
a meditative quiet

hear myself as loud
wonder what I
surround.

Pin Prick 82

The clown stares
into my eyes
decides
he'll no longer
cry.

My laughter
dies.

Pin Prick 83

I watch the news
eat mushroom soup

chopped fungus
cooked and condensed
pressed into a can

easily heated
simple to forget.

Pin Prick 84

Gentle curled knuckles caress jaw
shoulders relax, hand pulls back
eyes close

sigh

muscles tense, fingers tighten
knuckles shock eyes wide
mouth sprays blood, hand
follows through, fingers
relax

gently curled knuckles
caress jaw...

Pin Prick 85

The snake slides around itself
colourful skin kaleidoscoping
into a mass of light and dark
conflicting patterns
until the branch
that bears its weight
breaks.

Pin Prick 86

Near dawn I hear a leaf unfurl
look up in time to see it
flatten.

Its green is bright
unblemished quivering.
The sound already silent.

I close my eyes, slow
my breath, feel my mouth
start to smile.

Index of First Lines

Recent Quattro Poetry Books

Under the Mulberry Tree edited by James Deahl
Come Cold River by Karen Connelly
Beyond Mudtown by Rob Rolfe
And the cat says… by Susan L. Helwig
Against the Flight of Spring by Allan Briesmaster
The Rules of the Game by Ludwig Zeller
Too Much Love by Gianna Patriarca
parterre by elías carlo
Night-Eater by Patricia Young
Fermata by Dennison Smith
Little Empires by Robert Colman
nunami by Barbara Landry
One False Move by Tim Conley
Where the Terror Lies by Chantel Lavoie
Something Small To Carry Home by Isa Milman